A CHILD'S INTRODUCTION TO

The Nutcracker

A CHILD'S INTRODUCTION TO

The Nutcracker

The Story, Music, Costumes, and
Choreography of the Fairy Tale Ballet

HEATHER ALEXANDER

Illustrated by AMÉLIE VIDELO

BLACK DOG
& LEVENTHAL
PUBLISHERS
NEW YORK

Black Dog & Leventhal Publishers
Hachette Book Group
1290 Avenue of the Americas
New York, NY 10104

www.hachettebookgroup.com
www.blackdogandleventhal.com

First Edition: October 2021

Black Dog & Leventhal Publishers is an imprint of Perseus Books, LLC, a subsidiary of Hachette Book Group, Inc. The Black Dog & Leventhal Publishers name and logo are trademarks of Hachette Book Group, Inc.

The publisher is not responsible for websites (or their content) that are not owned by the publisher.

The Hachette Speakers Bureau provides a wide range of authors for speaking events.
To find out more, go to www.HachetteSpeakersBureau.com or call (866) 376-6591.

Print book interior design by Katie Benezra.

Library of Congress Cataloging-in-Publication Data
Names: Alexander, Heather, 1967– author.
Title: A child's introduction to The nutcracker : the story, music, costumes, and choreography of the fairy tale ballet / Heather Alexander.
Description: First edition. | New York : Black Dog & Leventhal Publishers, 2021. | Includes index. | Audience: Ages 8–12 | Summary: "A charmingly illustrated exploration of The Nutcracker ballet, from the story to the characters to the music, for kids aged 8–12 to enjoy" —Provided by publisher.
Identifiers: LCCN 2020048748 (print) | LCCN 2020048749 (ebook) | ISBN 9780762475124 (hardcover) | ISBN 9780762475131 (ebook)
Subjects: LCSH: Nutcracker (Choreographic work)—Juvenile literature.
Classification: LCC GV1790.N8 A48 2021 (print) | LCC GV1790.N8 (ebook) | DDC 792.8/42—dc23
LC record available at https://lccn.loc.gov/2020048748
LC ebook record available at https://lccn.loc.gov/2020048749

ISBNs: 978-0-7624-7512-4 (hardcover), 978-0-7624-7513-1 (ebook)

Printed in China

APS

10 9 8 7 6 5 4 3 2 1

For Jane Stine and Susan Lurie, who taught me that everything is beautiful at the ballet.

Special thanks to Jennifer Fisher, Professor of Dance, University of California, Irvine, as well as Dan Halpern, Simon Lipskar, Elizabeth Moulthrop, Lisa Tenaglia, Joe Davidson, Katie Benezra, and Betsy Hulsebosch.

Contents

Everything Nutcracker!

Someone once described ballet as "dreaming on your feet"—and that's exactly what *The Nutcracker* experience is every year for dancers, children, and the child that still lives inside all adults.

What is *The Nutcracker*?

The Nutcracker is an extremely famous ballet that's become a beloved holiday tradition. Every year, hundreds of ballet companies and schools on every continent (except Antarctica) perform this two-act, fairy-tale ballet. The music, written by composer Pyotr Ilyich Tchaikovsky, is recognized around the world. For many kids (and adults, too), *The Nutcracker* serves as a first introduction to ballet, to an orchestra, and to classical music.

What is ballet?

A ballet is an elegant and graceful form of dance with set positions, techniques, and footwork patterns. It takes many years of training and practice to master them all. Ballet dancers are beautiful artists, but they're also athletes.

How is a ballet different from a play or a musical?

In a ballet, you won't hear words like you do in a play or a musical. The dancers don't speak or sing. They use *only* their bodies to tell a story.

Is *The Nutcracker* a ballet or a story?

It's both. It started out as a short story. Then, a ballet company in Russia decided to adapt—or adjust—this story to create a ballet. Books and stories are often adapted into movies, musicals, and ballets. Some famous examples are Harry Potter (book to movie), *Wicked* (book to musical), and *The Sleeping Beauty* (fairy tale to ballet).

Why is *The Nutcracker* called a story ballet?

Because it tells a story! The ballet tells the story of a young girl who receives a nutcracker doll on Christmas Eve and the magical journey she takes to wondrous places.

The Nutcracker in 45 Words—Go!

Christmas party. Godfather brings Nutcracker for Clara. Brother breaks it. Clara sleeps. Midnight. Tree grows. Mice appear. Mouse King battles Nutcracker. Clara throws slipper at Mouse King. Nutcracker becomes Prince. Snowstorm. Land of Sweets. Meet Sugar Plum Fairy. Entertainment by Sweets. Time to go home.

Is every production of *The Nutcracker* the same?

Never. There are so, so many versions. Some are slightly different, and some are extremely different. That's why the production your cousin dances in their hometown may have different characters or a different ending than the production you watch in your hometown. The details of the story change from ballet company to ballet company, and so do the steps, scenery, and costumes. The one thing that almost always stays the same is the music.

What's *The Nutcracker* about?

Turn the page to read the story . . .

Because every production is different, the ballet steps, characters, and plot points described and illustrated in this book may not appear in the same way (or at all) in a production you see. A lot of descriptions in this book rely upon the version choreographed by George Balanchine, but you will find several other versions woven in, as well.

The Story

It was Christmas Eve. In the twilight's soft glow, the town's streets glistened with gently falling snow. Icicles hung from rooftops, and frost-dusted wreaths decorated doorways. Last-minute shoppers tightened their woolen scarves and buttoned their collars against the swirling wind. Everyone hurried home, arms laden with wrapped packages and sugar-spun sweets.

In Clara's house, the fireplace burned warm and bright. The aroma of cinnamon and peppermint floated down the hall from the kitchen. Holiday excitement filled the air. The familiar notes of a favorite melody played beyond the parlor's large double doors.

Balanced atop a wooden chair, Clara peeked through the door's keyhole.

Her parents were inside preparing for the family's wondrous party. They had instructed her and her brother, Fritz, to wait patiently in the hallway. But Christmas Eve was the most exciting day of the year. More exciting than her birthday and the first day of summer put together! How could she possibly be patient when sparkle and magic lay beyond these doors?

"What do you see?" Fritz asked, tugging impatiently on the hem of his older sister's dress. "Is the tree beautiful? Are there toys?"

"I don't know." Clara pressed her eye to the keyhole again.

A garland of holly. The sleeve of her mother's fancy blue dress. Glittering tinsel.

The keyhole was too tiny to glimpse much more. Clara stepped down, frustrated.

Fritz scrambled onto the chair, eager for his turn. He pressed his ear to the keyhole. "I think I hear Father. He's saying—"

At that moment, the doorbell rang.

The butler answered it, and a flurry of stomping feet and voices filled the foyer. The guests had arrived. Hats, gloves, and heavy coats were shed. The women fluffed their colorful skirts. The men straightened their ties. The children raced down the hallway as they all made their way, laughing and talking, to the closed parlor doors.

Fritz jumped off the chair, eagerly greeting the boys from his class. One boy started a game of tag, and they raced about, darting among the merry adults. Clara hugged each of her friends. Everyone was so dressed up! She admired their pretty hair ribbons and shiny shoes.

A silver bell chimed, and the large doors were finally flung open.

"Welcome, welcome!" Clara and Fritz's parents cried, ushering in their guests.

The parlor glowed with golden candlelight and was fragrant with pine. For a moment, Clara simply stood and stared openmouthed at the towering evergreen that occupied the center of the room. Hundreds of

delicate glass balls and strands of white lights twinkled on its branches. Candy canes, foil-covered chocolates, marzipan stars, and gingerbread animals decorated it, too. And spread out at the very base of the tree were piles of shiny presents in every shape and size.

Clara let out a squeal of delight and raced over to examine them. The other children had already gathered round, pointing out dolls and drums.

"Look at these!" Fritz bent over a squadron of toy soldiers. He jumped up and marched, as if he, too, were a soldier. Then he spotted a hobbyhorse on a stick and set off at a gallop around the tree.

Clara peered through a brass kaleidoscope, entranced by the twirling colors inside.

Lively music played, and the adults paired off to dance. Tiny iced cakes set upon silver trays were offered to the guests. Fritz reached up and grabbed three. Clara thought to scold him, but just then a hush fell over the room.

An old man appeared in the doorway.

He was tall and thin and dressed in black from head to toe. Tufts of white hair stuck out from the sides of his otherwise bald head. A patch covered his right eye, giving him a sinister look. He gazed about with his one good eye, frowning until he spotted Clara. Then he smiled.

"Godfather Drosselmeyer!" Placing the kaleido-scope back under the tree, Clara flung herself into his open arms.

He gave her a quick hug, then announced, "I have presents."

Clara clapped. Her godfather always gave the best gifts! He was a clever toymaker, but the people in town whispered that Drosselmeyer was also a magician. They said he made his toys move by enchanting them with magic.

But Clara didn't believe that. She'd visited his workshop and knew about the hidden gears and springs he used to build his toys. Clara was very interested in how machines worked. How *everything* worked, really. That was why she was Drosselmeyer's favorite. Well, that, and because Fritz always broke every new toy he got.

Now Drosselmeyer dragged two enormous boxes into the center of the room. One had a big yellow bow. The other had a big purple bow. Everyone circled round, curious. What marvelous toys had Drosselmeyer invented this year?

Drosselmeyer stepped forward and opened the boxes. Clara leaped back. Two life-sized dolls walked out on their own! One was Harlequin, and the other, Columbine. They both wore colorful, diamond-patterned satin

outfits. Drosselmeyer placed a metal crank into each of their backs to wind both of them up. Once, twice, three times—and then the mechanical dolls began to dance together.

Once the dolls finished their performance, Clara's godfather pulled her aside. "I have a special present for you."

She followed Drosselmeyer's gaze to the tree. He nodded, and she hurried over to find a small doll tucked underneath. It was a soldier, carved out of wood, standing stiffly at attention. It wore a painted-blue coat and a tall, red hat. Its head seemed too big for its body. She stared at it, and for a moment, she imagined its painted eyes were actually looking at her. She smiled, half expecting the little soldier to smile back.

"It's a nutcracker," explained Drosselmeyer. "Let me show you."

He produced a walnut and pulled a lever to open the wooden doll's jaw wide. He popped the nut inside, pushed the lever, and—*wham!*—the shell cracked in half. The nut fell out, and Drosselmeyer ate it!

Clara gave it a try. She cracked one nut in the mechanical jaw. Then another and another, handing them out to her friends.

"Oh, Godfather!" Clara hugged the nutcracker. "I love him! Thank you—"

"I want him!" Fritz was suddenly by her side. "Let me try!"

"Don't be so rough." Clara moved her doll away from his grasping hands.

"Give him here!" Fritz lunged at the nutcracker. He grabbed it by the legs.

Clara held tight onto its head.

Fritz pulled. Clara pulled. But Fritz pulled harder, and then *CRACK!* The nutcracker's wooden jaw split apart.

"You broke it!" She whirled on her little brother.

Fritz's face reddened with embarrassment, and he raced off.

Clara choked back tears. She knew she was

too old to cry over a toy, but she was crying for the nutcracker, not for herself. It was as if she could feel the nutcracker's pain. She cradled him in her arms.

Drosselmeyer reached down and gently untied the blue ribbon Clara wore in her hair. He used it to bandage the nutcracker's broken jaw. Then he placed the injured doll back under the tree.

"Let him rest tonight," he told Clara. He brushed away the tear trickling down her cheek.

Clara nodded and glanced into her godfather's warm gaze. Was that a mysterious twinkle she spotted in his eye? Before Clara could give it another thought, the music started up again, and everyone glided across the floor for a final dance. The party was ending.

Clara didn't want to leave her nutcracker, but her mother said it would be rude not to see her friends out. The frosty night air rushed through the front door, and she wrapped her arms around herself and

wished them good-bye. Then Clara and Fritz were quickly ushered upstairs to get ready for bed.

Yawning, Clara slipped under the covers. But she couldn't sleep. She worried about her nutcracker. She kept thinking about him, alone and injured.

Quietly, she pushed her feet into her slippers and softly made her way down the dimly lit stairs and into the parlor. The house was silent, except for the ticking of the large grandfather clock that stood by the window. The strings of lights on the tree still glowed,

but the rest of the house was blanketed in darkness. Her family was asleep.

Clara lifted her nutcracker into her arms, rocking him gently. She curled up on the sofa with him and hummed a holiday melody. Her eyelids soon grew heavy. She lay her head down, falling into a deep slumber.

BONG! BONG! BONG!

The big clock chimed midnight and startled Clara awake.

She rubbed her eyes. Why was she downstairs on the floor in the parlor? She sat up as memories of the party and her nutcracker trickled back to her.

And then she gasped.

Right before her, the Christmas tree started to grow. She watched in astonishment as it rose bigger and bigger! Its large branches stretched up and out. It didn't stop growing until the top pushed against the parlor ceiling.

But wait! Clara's heart fluttered. The tree wasn't the only thing growing and growing. The toys underneath were growing, too!

Fritz's toy soldiers were becoming as big as real people. And so was her nutcracker!

Just as the soldiers neared their full height, she heard the scratching. And the sound of scurrying feet.

Mice! Mice! Everywhere! They scuttled from one side of the room to the other. But these mice weren't ordinary mice. They were taller than Clara, and wider, too. She pulled her knees to her chest and held her breath.

A mouse even more enormous than the others scampered forward. It was the Mouse King. He wore a gold crown and brandished a curved sword. The sword's blade glinted in the lights shining from the enormous tree.

The Nutcracker leaped to meet the Mouse King. His army of toy soldiers, now fully grown, joined in. As the Mouse King swung his sword, the Nutcracker pulled his own sword from his belt.

The battle began. Drums beat, and trumpets blared. The mice surged forward. The soldiers thrust swords at the mice. The mice pushed the soldiers down. The soldiers fired cannons at the mice. Then more mice appeared. And more.

Clara stood for a better view. *Oh, no!* The Mouse King had the Nutcracker cornered. As he raised his sword to attack, another mouse snatched the Nutcracker's sword. The Nutcracker searched urgently for an escape. But he was surrounded.

"Get away!" Clara shouted at the mice, desperate to help Nutcracker. She pulled off her left slipper and hurled it with all her might at the Mouse King.

Thwack!

Much to her surprise, she hit him squarely between the eyes. The Mouse King toppled to the ground.

Eyes wide, Clara watched in horror as the mice gathered around their fallen leader. Defeated, they scooped him up and carried his limp body away.

Clara sank back onto the sofa. She lowered her head, trying to slow her thudding heart.

"Thank you. You saved my life."

Clara gazed up and stifled a gasp. The Nutcracker had transformed into a prince. His warm brown eyes met hers, and he smiled.

"Come with me to the Land of Sweets." The prince held out his hand.

Clara took it, and together they began to walk, and as they did, the parlor faded away. Her Christmas tree transformed into an entire pine forest. Snow flurries drifted from the sky, swirling gently in the night air.

But soon the snow began to fall harder. The wind gusted. The snowflakes danced circles around them. A blizzard blanketed the forest in silver and white. Clara glanced down and noticed she was wearing only one slipper, but strangely enough, her foot wasn't cold. She raised her head to the sky and then twirled until she was dizzy. Thick white flakes landed on Clara's nose and eyelashes.

"This way." The prince guided her out of the blinding snowstorm.

And into the Land of Sweets.

They walked on a candy-cobblestone path, passing enormous lollipop trees. Gumdrops dotted cotton-candy bushes. Majestic fountains sent up arches of bubbling butterscotch and sparkling pink lemonade. *Can this truly be real?* Clara wondered. Gingerbread

houses with toffee-tile roofs dripped with pastel icing. Tulips and roses grew soft taffy petals. Everything here was made from sugar. It took Clara's breath away.

"Greetings!" The sweetest woman Clara had ever seen appeared before them. She wore a pale green tutu. Her hair was the same soft pink as her shiny satin slippers.

"This is the Sugar Plum Fairy," said the prince.

Clara curtsied, for it was clear this woman ruled the Land of Sweets.

The prince told her of their battle with the Mouse King and their victory.

"You are both very brave," the Sugar Plum Fairy said.

Clara blushed. She'd never been called brave by someone so important before.

"We must celebrate you." The Sugar Plum Fairy invited them to sit side by side on two magnificent

golden thrones. Her helpers brought them ice cream sundaes and fizzy cherry drinks. And then the entertainment began. All the delights of the Land of Sweets would perform.

Spanish Hot Chocolate, Arabian Coffee, and Chinese Tea took the stage, one after the other, having traveled far from different lands. They pirouetted and leaped high in the air. Next, peppermint candy canes jumped through hoops, and marzipan shepherdesses played delicate reed pipes while spinning on their toes.

Clara and the prince clapped with delight. The prince offered a cupcake to Clara, but she waved it away. A large woman with a tall pouf of silver hair was gliding toward them. Clara moved to the edge of her throne. It was Mother Ginger, and she wore a hoop skirt that was as wide as a house!

Clara heard a rustling coming from under Mother Ginger's skirt. And then she was sure she heard a giggle. *How strange!*

Suddenly Mother Ginger's skirt parted like a curtain, and a bright-eyed child popped out! And then another tumbled out. And another and another. Eight clown-children, or polichinelles, giggled and danced about. Clara waved to them, and they waved happily back at her. When they were done dancing, Mother Ginger gathered her children back under her skirt and whisked them away.

At that moment, the taffy flowers turned their faces toward the sun and burst to life. Their pastel petals opened and closed as they began to waltz. Spinning quickly across the floor, the blossoms whirled into a blur of color. The shimmering Dewdrop Fairy joined in the dance, gathering the flowers into a lovely bouquet.

For the final performance, the graceful Sugar Plum Fairy danced with her dashing Cavalier. The Sugar Plum Fairy glided as if she were dancing on clouds. She raised one long leg to the sky and balanced on the toe of her other leg for the longest time. And then she lowered her leg and began to spin—faster, faster, faster. She leaped into the Cavalier's waiting arms, and Clara was on her feet, applauding.

If only someday I could dance like the Sugar Plum Fairy, she thought. *And live in a place as sweet as this.*

Clara began to dance a few steps of her own, but the prince stopped her. It was time for them to go. They climbed into a sled pulled by magical reindeer. As the sled rose up into the night sky, Clara waved good-bye to the Land of Sweets. Flurries began to fall again, and she pulled a velvet blanket she'd found in the sled around her.

They drifted through the night and the stars.

And Clara closed her eyes.

When she opened them, it was morning, and she was once again curled up on the parlor sofa. Someone had covered her with a soft blanket in the night. She pushed it back and slowly sat up. The wooden nutcracker was tucked in beside her.

Clara held the doll up to the sun glinting through a small gap in the drapes. His ribbon bandage was mysteriously gone. The nutcracker was fully healed and as good as new.

Clara rubbed her eyes. *Had it all been a dream?*

She heard her parents and Fritz stir upstairs. Soon they'd be down for breakfast. She hurried across the room to the tall bookcase. Balancing on a chair, she placed the nutcracker on the highest shelf, safely away from her brother. She stared at the nutcracker's painted face for a moment, willing him to come to life. But nothing happened.

Then she stepped down . . . and stumbled upon something on the floor.

Her left slipper!

She picked it up. *How curious. What is it doing all the way over here?*

Her heart began to pound, and she glanced up to her nutcracker.

And gave him a knowing smile.

From Book to Ballet

PAGE TO STAGE

The Nutcracker's journey from page to stage began in Germany in 1816, when author E. T. A. Hoffmann published a dark fairy tale called *The Nutcracker and the Mouse King*. The story combined real life with fantasy and featured a creepy seven-headed mouse king. In 1844, French author Alexandre Dumas (who also wrote *The Three Musketeers*) penned a new version of the story that was much less scary. He added more fantasy and took out a long flashback that explained how the prince turned into the nutcracker. He also changed the main character's name from Marie to Clara. He titled his fairy tale *The Tale of a Nutcracker.*

THE DYNAMIC DUO

Jump ahead almost fifty years. The Mariinsky Theater in St. Petersburg, Russia, was the center of the ballet world at the time. **Choreographer** (the person who makes up the dances) Marius Petipa and **composer** (the person who writes the music) Pyotr Ilyich Tchaikovsky have just staged the ballet *The Sleeping Beauty.* Critics gave it glowing reviews, and audiences gave it standing ovations. The dynamic duo of Petipa and Tchaikovsky decided to team up again to create another ballet.

The director of the theater, Ivan Vsevolozhsky, had the idea to turn Hoffmann's *Nutcracker* story into a ballet. He and Petipa spoke French, so they based the libretto on Dumas's version. (A libretto is the storyline of a ballet or opera.) Once the libretto was finished, Petipa wrote a rough description of all the dances. Then he handed Tchaikovsky detailed instructions that mapped out the exact music and tempo (that's the rhythm and speed) he wanted for each part of every dance, such as: "48 bars of great crescendo as Christmas tree rises." Tchaikovsky was the first well-known composer to write music for a ballet, and he was somewhat annoyed by Petipa's strict directions. Nevertheless, he brilliantly transformed them into majestic melodies that soared with imagination and emotion.

But it wasn't easy. From the beginning, Tchaikovsky had trouble figuring out how to balance the drama-heavy Act 1 with the lighter Act 2. He was also composing an opera, *Iolanta,* to be staged together with the ballet (back then, wealthy theatergoers watched long back-to-back performances). The scoring (that's the writing of the music) for both was going so slowly that Tchaikovsky had to ask for more time. Then, once he was finally able to begin work on Act 2 of *The Nutcracker,* his beloved sister Sasha died. He plunged into deep sadness and took a break from writing. But after a while, his memories of Sasha and their childhood together gave him the inspiration he needed to finish.

ISN'T IT SWEET?

After the score was completed—but before the ballet was performed—Tchaikovsky combined eight of his favorite melodies together in a piece he called *The Nutcracker Suite* (pronounced "sweet"). The St. Petersburg orchestra played it at a concert. Because the twenty-minute *Suite* was only supposed to be listened to, there were no dancers to watch. It was a ringing success.

OPENING NIGHT

Meanwhile, ballet rehearsals had begun. But before choreographing the dances, ballet master Petipa fell ill and his assistant Lev Ivanov had to take over. In December 1892, a sold-out crowd filled the Mariinsky Theater for opening night. Was the ballet a huge hit?

No! The reviews were mixed. Some critics liked it, but others didn't. They complained about having to wait until the very end for the Sugar Plum Fairy's magnificent dance (remember, they'd already sat through an entire opera!). Some reviewers frowned at the casting of real children in lead roles, which hadn't been done before. One wrote, "In the first scene the entire stage is filled with children, who run about, blow their whistles, hop and jump, are naughty, and interfere with the oldsters dancing. In large amounts this is unbearable." But many reviewers praised the dancers' skill, the "Waltz of the Snowflakes"

choreography, the costumes, and the stage design.

Everyone loved Tchaikovsky's score, although some wondered if it was "dance-able." Up until this point, the main job of ballet music had been to keep a strong, simple beat for the dancers. Critics wondered if Tchaikovsky's richly layered music was, in fact, too good and complex for a ballet. Even though the tsar (the emperor of Russia) summoned Tchaikovsky to the royal box at the theater to congratulate him, Tchaikovsky was upset by the generally negative reaction and announced he'd never compose music for a ballet again. A year later, he died. He passed away believing his ballet was a failure. He never knew it would be become his best-known, most popular, and most beloved work.

A person who is a fan of the ballet is called a balletomane.

COMING OUT OF ITS SHELL

The Nutcracker wasn't very popular in Russia and, for decades, was only performed on and off (and not during Christmastime, like it is now in the United States and Canada). The ballet's first international performance was at the Sadler's Wells Theater in London in 1934. It was staged by Russian dancers and choreographers who'd fled to Europe after the 1917 Russian Revolution (when the tsar was overthrown and the Communists took over the government). The dancers had smuggled notes for the choreography out of the country with them.

ALEXANDRA DANILOVA
AND GEORGE BALANCHINE

In 1940, *The Nutcracker* came to America. Ballets Russes de Monte-Carlo—a European dance company made up of many former Russian dancers—toured the United States. Their traveling dance company was the first to introduce ballet in small cities and towns across the country. They performed a shortened, one-act version of *The Nutcracker,* and Americans became fascinated with the Russian style of ballet.

During the same year, Walt Disney used the *Nutcracker* music in his blockbuster movie *Fantasia.* On the screen, animated flowers, fairies, and fish whirled like nature's version of ballet dancers. Some figures were actually based on films of Ballet Russe dancers. American audiences began to recognize and hum Tchaikovsky's enchanted melodies.

FIRST FULL U.S. PERFORMANCE

The first full-length, two-act professional production of *The Nutcracker* in the United States was presented on Christmas Eve in 1944 by the San Francisco Ballet. The choreographer was Willam Christensen. Russian dancers Alexandra Danilova and George Balanchine were on tour in the U.S. at that time and suggested he stage this ballet to attract a holiday audience. But when Christensen began to map out the steps, he realized he had a big problem. He'd never seen the entire ballet! He had no idea what was supposed to happen onstage. There was no *How to Nutcracker* instruction manual—and home video hadn't been invented yet. Christensen asked Danilova and Balanchine for their advice since they'd danced in the original production in Russia. Balanchine told him to just do his own thing and not worry about matching the original. But Danilova shared her memories and showed Christensen some of the steps. Christensen cast his sister-in-law, Gisella Caccialanza, as the Sugar Plum Fairy.

GISELLA
CACCIALANZA

DIY COSTUMES

Christensen's ballet company did not have much money. They gave a nineteen-year-old company member named Russell Hartley their entire budget of $1,000 to buy supplies and to design all 143 costumes. Hartley had to get crafty! He purchased red velvet curtains at a Goodwill store for $10 and used the fabric to sew jackets for every male partygoer in the first scene. He found rhinestone jewelry and fake flowers for $5 at Goodwill, too. At this time, World War II was being fought overseas, and every American was only allowed to buy a few yards of fabric each month so the military would have enough to make the millions of uniforms they needed. The dancers contributed their ration of fabric to the show. Many sewed their own tutus and costumes at home.

STANDING O

Audiences gave the performance standing ovations—and the critics cheered. The San Francisco Ballet began to stage the ballet year after year, almost immediately. In 1951, Christensen moved to Salt Lake City, Utah, to start a new company called Ballet West, and he brought his version of *The Nutcracker* with him. His production holds the world record for the longest-running yearly performance of *The Nutcracker.*

THE BIG APPLE

However, the credit for turning *The Nutcracker* into an American holiday tradition goes to George Balanchine. Balanchine was a ballet dancer who'd grown up performing the parts of a mouse, the Nutcracker Prince, a candy cane dancer, and the Mouse King when he was a student in St. Petersburg. Now that he was the founder and choreographer of the New York City Ballet, he made his own version, combining his Russian past with new elements he thought an American audience would enjoy. When it was suggested he put on a shortened version,

Balanchine replied, "If I do anything, it will be full-length and expensive."

Balanchine believed in going all out. He remembered Christmases back home filled with merriment, warmth, and chocolate galore. He wanted to bring that rush of sugar onto the stage. And he wanted an *enormous* tree that would grow and grow. But his budget for the entire production was $40,000. Building an enormous tree onstage and making it grow would cost $25,000, which meant he'd have to spend over half of his budget on one tree. The person in charge of the money told Balanchine he'd have to do without the tree. Balanchine refused and replied,

"*The Nutcracker is* the tree." Guess what? The budget ended up being increased, and the tree stayed.

Balanchine created most of the choreography for his version himself (just liked he'd once told Christensen to do). His imaginative and dynamic footwork brought the story to life and audiences to the edges of their seats. He expanded the children's roles and cast real children to dance them. He believed it was important for all young dance students to have the thrilling experience of performing on a stage, just as he'd once done. And, unlike the audiences in Russia, Americans adored seeing children onstage.

George Balanchine's The Nutcracker premiered on February 2, 1954, at City Center in New York City.

Three years later, the ballet was broadcast live on national television. For the first time, families all over the country could sit in their living rooms and share the experience. In 1977, the ballet was once again aired on television for all to enjoy. This time it was Mikhail Baryshnikov's American Ballet Theater's version.

Ballet schools in the U.S. and Canada began staging their own performances, some influenced by Balanchine's choreography, some by Christensen's and others. The ballet became more and more popular, and it wasn't long before *The Nutcracker* had turned into a treasured holiday tradition and phenomenon throughout North America.

Choreographers: The Big Three

What Does a Choreographer Do?

A choreographer creates the dance steps. They figure out not only the positions of the legs and feet, but the positions of the arms, hands, head, and body. They must decide how the steps flow into one another, how the dancers move about the stage, and how best to show off each dancer's talent. Choreographers are inspired by music and story. Every choreographer has their own style. What's your style? Try to choreograph your own thirty-second dance!

MARIUS PETIPA (1818–1910)

Choreographer Marius Petipa is sometimes called "the father of classical ballet." Born in Marseilles, France, Petipa came from a family of dancers and was trained by his father, who was a professional ballet dancer and choreographer. Petipa made his first stage appearance as a young child in a ballet staged by his father. Petipa grew up to become a principal (lead) dancer, performing all over Europe and the U.S. In 1847, he moved to St. Petersburg, Russia, to join the Imperial Theater's impressive ballet company. He fell in love with Russia and lived there for the rest of his life. He became an instructor and was eventually named

Premier Ballet Master at the famed Mariinsky Theater. During his lifetime, Petipa choreographed over sixty full-length ballets, including *The Sleeping Beauty*, *Don Quixote*, and *La Bayadère*. Marius Petipa's talent is a big reason why the 1890s has been called "the Golden Age of Russian Ballet."

LEV IVANOV (1834–1901)

Lev Ivanov lived his whole life in Marius Petipa's shadow. He choreographed *The Nutcracker* and much of *Swan Lake,* yet he never achieved anywhere near the same level of fame as Petipa did. Born in Moscow, Russia, Ivanov started taking classes at the Imperial School of Ballet in St. Petersburg at age ten. Ivanov had an incredible natural talent for music. If he heard a ballet's music just once, he could immediately play the entire score by ear on the piano without any sheet music or instruction. But his ballet instructors didn't applaud this. They pushed him to transfer to the music school. Ivanov refused—he wanted to dance, not study music theory. At age eighteen, he became a member of the Mariinsky ballet company. Because of his excellent memory, he was often cast as the understudy for the lead roles. And guess who danced many of those lead roles? Marius Petipa! When Petipa was promoted to ballet master, Ivanov rose to become principal dancer. In 1885, he became Petipa's teaching and choreography assistant. When Petipa became ill, Ivanov ended up choreographing *The Nutcracker,* and his choreography was extremely musical. In the "Waltz of the Snowflakes," he created a winter wonderland snowstorm that paired perfectly with Tchaikovsky's swirling notes. At the time, Ivanov was not publicly applauded or much admired. In fact, only Petipa's name appeared on the posters for *The Nutcracker*'s first production. Despite a long, successful career in ballet, Ivanov died in poverty.

FUN FACT

An understudy needs to know every step just in case they must fill in at the last minute for a principal dancer who is unable to perform.

GEORGE BALANCHINE
(1904–1983)

George Balanchine was born Gyorgy Balanchivadze in 1904 in St. Petersburg, Russia. His parents were both musicians, and young George was a very talented piano player. When he was nine years old, his mother dragged him along to his older sister Tamara's audition for the Imperial School of Ballet. The ballet teacher spotted a bored-looking George sitting off to the side. He asked him to hop, skip, and twirl. George was unsure why—*he* didn't want to be a dancer. But he did it anyway.

The ballet teacher read out the names of the students who had been chosen to attend the school. Tamara wasn't on the list. But George was! His mother and sister left him to live at the strict and demanding ballet school, where he would be trained along with twenty-nine other boys. That first night he was so upset that he ran away, but he was quickly found and brought back. George was going be a dancer, whether he liked it or not. For the next year, he took ballet lessons for hours and hours each day. But he still didn't want to dance. Then, one day, everything changed.

In his second year of school, George was given a small role as a cupid in Tchaikovsky's ballet *The Sleeping Beauty.* As he waited to go onstage, he watched the performance from the wings (the sides of the stage). He loved the beautiful costumes and the bright makeup. He was carried away by the sounds of the orchestra, and for the first time he saw how dance and music came together. And suddenly dance made sense to him. With his body, he would be able to show an audience how music made him feel. From then on, he became a passionate dancer.

World War I and the Russian Revolution took place while George was still at the ballet school. Times grew very hard. He and the other students had to search and beg for scraps of food and clothing. But through it all, he never stopped dancing. He graduated and began to choreograph his own pieces. George's dances were dramatic, but unlike ballets of the past, they didn't tell stories. He felt an audience would better focus on the dancing if they didn't have to follow a plot.

Six years after the end of World War I, in 1924, George joined a group of dancers on a tour of European cities. He was eager to escape the hardships and new Communist government in his country, which was now called the Soviet Union. While abroad, the director of the Ballets Russes invited George to move to Monte Carlo and choreograph ballets for the company. George took the job and changed his last name to the more European-sounding Balanchine.

Balanchine traveled from company to company and choreographed new ballets all around Europe. In 1933, a wealthy American named Lincoln Kirstein sought him out. Kirstein was sure America had much undiscovered ballet talent, and he wanted someone creative to start an American company. He chose Balanchine.

Balanchine sailed to New York City and opened the School of American Ballet. He was also busy choreographing for Broadway shows, Hollywood films, and even the circus (he once tried—unsuccessfully—to teach elephants to do ballet!). In 1948, he co-founded the New York City Ballet and focused his full attention on making his company a success.

Balanchine Americanized classical ballet, making it more modern, lighter, and faster. He combined free-spirited American athleticism with Russian elegance and graceful technique. Many different dance styles, including Broadway, jazz, and African, influenced him. His collaboration with famous dancers such as Josephine Baker and Katherine Dunham led him to incorporate aspects of their moves, such as syncopated rhythm, angled arms and flexed wrists, and mobile torsos, into his unique choreography. He paid close attention to details, especially to the position of a dancer's head. He stressed musical timing and,

above all, Balanchine wanted his dancers to have a connection with the audience and be as passionate about dance as he was. "Dancers have to be strong-willed," he once said. "They must put all their mind and body into it. You can't be half and half."

Balanchine choreographed a ballet called *The Firebird* and cast a young Native dancer named Maria Tallchief in the role of a magic bird, turning her into a star.

Balanchine decided to stage an elaborate, full-length ballet to attract bigger audiences. He chose *The Nutcracker* and appeared in the role of Drosselmeyer. He loved this role, because it allowed him to act onstage. His *Nutcracker* was a hit. In fact, *George Balanchine's The Nutcracker* has played in New York City every Christmas since its premiere in 1954. George Balanchine died at the age of seventy-nine. The School of American Ballet still continues to teach using his techniques, and his ballets are still performed all over the world.

All About Ballet

THE BEGINNINGS OF BALLET

Ballet had a regal start in the palaces of Italy during the 1400s as entertainment for royalty. When Italian noblewoman Catherine de Medici (1519–1589) married France's King Henry II, she had the Italian court dancers travel to France to perform. Catherine once even paid for a six-hour ballet-and-song extravaganza and invited ten thousand royal guests! The elite of France quickly fell in love with ballet.

Ballet comes from the Italian word *ballare*, which means "to dance."

Italian and French court dancers performed in masks, towering headdresses, frilly pantaloons, heels, and elaborate costumes. As you can imagine, these heavy clothes made it hard to move, so the steps stayed simple—mostly small turns, curtsies, and promenades. It was all very, very formal. These dances were called *ballet de cour,* or court dances.

THE SUN KING

Ballet was brought to new heights in France under the reign of King Louis XIV (1638–1715). King Louis Quatorze ("fourteen" in French) was a dancer himself with his own private dance tutor. He received the nickname "Sun King" after he performed the role of Apollo, the Greek sun god, in a magnificent headgear shaped like the rays of the sun. In 1661, the king called for the world's first dance academy to open in Paris. He instructed ballet masters to write out strict rules that dancers should follow, including the five basic positions. The ballet rules were shared with dance teachers throughout Europe. This is why most ballet words are in French.

Only nobles could attend France's Académie Royale de Danse, but soon other dancers began to perform on public stages for ordinary people. With the dancers now raised above the crowd, audiences had a better view of their feet. Ballet steps grew more complicated. Because dancers had to face forward toward the king during the early years of ballet, they danced with their hips and legs turned out. The turned-out position allowed dancers to move easily in any direction. Fencers also stand in this posture for the same reason.

FUN FACT

Louis XIV was not yet five years old when he became king!

KING LOUIS XIV

GIRL POWER

Even though dance had moved from the palaces to the stage, female dancers were at first banned from performing in public. Men danced the female roles, wearing wigs and long skirts. Mademoiselle De Lafontaine broke the rule in 1681, becoming the first woman to dance on a professional stage. She had a super-tight corset cinched around her waist and heavy bell-shaped skirts that were the fashion back then, so her dancing may not have been all that fabulous. Nevertheless, her bravery paved the way for the future of female ballet dancers.

Marie Sallé was the next to shake up the dance world when she appeared onstage without a mask or wig in the 1730s. She allowed her long hair to flow naturally, and she conveyed emotion with her face as she danced. Instead of wearing a big hoop dress that hid her body, she twirled in a simple muslin tunic that showed her calves and ankles! Her rebellion was scandalous at the time, but soon other dancers followed her lead. Finally free to really move, female dancers' skill and footwork quickly stole the spotlight from the men.

ALWAYS EVOLVING

In the 1800s, the center of the ballet world shifted from Paris to Russia. Russian choreographers and composers created expressive ballets based on dramatic stories, often from fairy tales. *The Nutcracker* (1892), along with *The Sleeping Beauty* (1890) and *Swan Lake* (1875), are some of the best-known Russian ballets.

Over the next century, more and more ballet companies were formed throughout the world. Modern ballets were staged, and classical ballets were reimagined. Ballet absorbed influences from different cultures and attracted new, diverse audiences and dancers. Ballet is a living art, so it continues to evolve in exciting ways with new choreography, costumes, and even moving from the stage onto the computer screen in your own home and school.

MADEMOISELLE
DE LAFONTAINE

Step Right Up

FIRST POSITION

FOURTH POSITION

SECOND POSITION

FIFTH POSITION

THIRD POSITION

Ballet is beautiful, but it's also difficult. There are set positions for the feet, arms, and body that all dancers must learn, practice, and master before performing onstage.

THE FIVE POSITIONS

Every step in ballet uses one or more of five basic positions. All the positions are done with **turnout**. For proper turnout, a dancer must rotate their legs at the hips, so there is no strain on the knees.

Do ballet dancers point their toes to look pretty?

Most definitely, but that's not the only reason. Pointed toes complete the long line of the leg. By activating the muscles in their feet, a dancer can stretch their body longer and give it power. Here's a trick for powerful pointed toes—pretend you're shooting lightning bolts from your toes.

Dance Class

Dancers practice in large rooms called **studios**. Studios have big mirrors, so dancers can see the position of their bodies as they move. All ballet classes begin with warm-up exercises at the **barre**, a horizontal wooden bar fastened to the wall. Dancers hold on to it for support. After barre work, dancers will practice skills in the center of the room and across the floor.

Beginning Moves

Relevé means "to rise." A dancer keeps their legs straight and lifts their heels, bringing all their weight onto the balls of their turned-out feet.

Plié means "to bend." A dancer bends their knees outward to lower their body, while keeping their legs turned out from the hips.

Sauté means "to jump." A dancer begins in plié, jumps in the air while straightening their legs, then lands gracefully, back in plié.

Strike a Pose

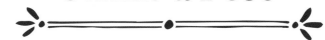

Arabesque has a dancer stand perfectly balanced on one leg while the other leg is stretched out in a straight line behind with the toes pointed. The arms are extended gracefully with a long line from fingertip to toe.

LOOK FOR IT

You can usually see a great example of an arabesque during the party scene, when Clara holds up her nutcracker doll.

Attitude is similar to the arabesque, but the knee of the raised leg is slightly bent.

Up in the Air

Jeté means "to throw." A jeté is a springing jump or leap, where the weight is thrown from one foot to the other.

Grand jeté means "a really big jeté"!

Tour jeté means "turning jump." A jeté is done while making a half turn in the air.

Tour en l'air means "turn in the air." It's a complete single, double, or triple turn in the air, usually from fifth position. Traditionally this is performed by a male dancer, but female dancers can also do them.

Spins and Twirls

Pirouette means "to whirl about." The dancer does a full spin on one leg, while the other leg is raised off the ground. The dancer may perform one rotation or many. A pirouette is done either *en dehors* (turning away from the supporting leg) or *en dedans* (turning toward the supporting leg).

LOOK FOR IT

Sometimes at the end of Act I, the snowflakes perform a series of *pirouettes enchaînement* (a whole bunch in a line or in a circle).

FUN FACT

In 2013, an eleven-year-old girl named Sophia Lucia broke the world record for the most pirouettes—she did 55 consecutive turns!

Fouetté means "whipped." As part of a pirouette, the dancer makes a quick whipping motion with their leg. Fouettés are most often done several at a time, using the one leg to whip out and propel each turn.

Why don't ballet dancers get dizzy when they spin?

Dancers have a trick called **spotting**. Before beginning to turn, a dancer finds a small object at eye level to focus on, such as the number "3" on a clock or a sign on a wall. They keep their eyes locked on that object as their body turns, whipping their head around at the very last moment and refocusing again on that same spot. If a dancer practices in front of a mirror, they will sometimes spot themselves.

Three Rules
(for Traditional Ballet)

☑ **Always, always turn out.**

☑ **Always point your toes if your feet are off the floor.**

☑ **Always stretch your leg out as far as it can go (unless your leg is supposed to be bent).**

On Pointe

In *The Nutcracker,* you'll see many dancers balance and twirl on the tips of their toes. This is called "en pointe" in French, or "on pointe" in English. Performing on pointe makes a dancer look as if they're magically floating on air.

Get to the Pointe

To dance on pointe, a dancer wears special shoes called pointe shoes or toe shoes. While these shoes may look dainty on the outside, don't be fooled. Inside, they're actually super-tough athletic equipment. It takes great mastery and strength to dance gracefully on pointe.

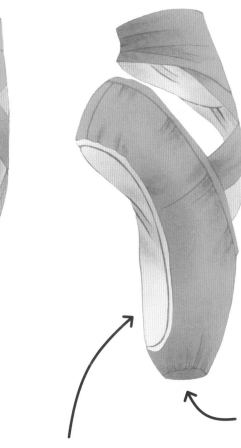

RIBBONS

The ribbons cross over the instep and wind around the ankles to hold the shoe on the foot. A dancer sews the ribbons onto the shoe to get the exact fit they like. They also attach a strip of elastic to the heel to keep it from slipping off.

SATIN
The shiny fabric covering the shoe.

SHANK
The shank is the shoe's stiff inner sole. A dancer must break in the shank to get a beautiful curve in their foot, called an arched foot.

BOX
The box at the tip of the shoe is made of layers of tightly packed fabric and paper hardened by glue. The box acts like a sturdy platform for the toes to balance upon. A dancer's core and leg muscles must be strong to help them support their full body weight on this tiny box. (Most dancers wrap and cushion their toes and feet with tape, cotton, or foam pads before putting on their pointe shoes.)

Pointed Questions

Why can't I dance on pointe in ballet slippers?

Ouch! Unless you have toes of steel, you'll badly injure your feet. Ballet slippers don't have nearly enough support.

Do boys wear pointe shoes?

Yes. Most classical ballets were choreographed with male dancers wearing soft ballet slippers, but more recent ballets feature male dancers on pointe.

When can a dancer go on pointe?

A dancer must wait until their ankles and entire body are strong enough, which is usually at age eleven or twelve, after at least a few years of training. All pointe dancers must learn the proper technique, so they don't hurt themselves.

What's the crumbly white powder a dancer rubs on their shoes?

It's called rosin, and it makes the shoes less slippery. Violinists also use rosin on their bows, and baseball pitchers use it to improve their grip on the ball.

If a dancer says their pointe shoes are "dead," what do they mean?

It's time for a new pair. Pointe shoes start out very stiff, and a dancer breaks them in by stepping on the box, pounding them against the wall, or jamming them in a door. But once the shoes get very comfy, they usually become too soft and "die." Then the dancer must get a new pair and break them in all over again.

How many pointe shoes does a professional dancer use in one season?

A principal dancer might go through hundreds of shoes in a season. The average life of a shoe is one to two weeks, but sometimes a pair may last for only a single performance!

What's the pointe shoe room?

Ballet companies often have a special room filled with hundreds of pointe shoes for their dancers' many performances. On the sole of some shoes, there's a stamped symbol, such as a cloverleaf or a heart. Each shoemaker has a special symbol to show who made that particular shoe.

HEEL TO TOES

In the early days of ballet, women danced in heeled shoes. Can you imagine pirouetting and leaping in heels? In the mid-1700s, French-Belgian dancer Marie Camargo was one of the first women to remove the heels from her dancing shoes. Other dancers quickly agreed this was the way to go. Then, in 1796, a dancer named Charles Didelot brought ballet to new heights when he invented a "flying machine." Hidden wires and pulleys raised a dancer up onto her toes and held her there, before whizzing her into the air. Audiences went wild for this balancing act!

FUN FACT

Legend has it, Taglioni was so popular that after her last performance in Russia in 1842, a group of her fans bought a pair of her ballet shoes for a huge amount of money, cooked them into a stew topped with a special sauce, and then ate them!

In 1832, Italian ballerina Maria Taglioni was the first to dance a full-length ballet on pointe. She appeared magical, as if she were a creature from another world floating across the stage. Taglioni showed that pointe was not just an athletic feat but an artistic way to poetically tell a story.

Dressed to Dance

When you think of ballet, you probably think tutu and tights. But that's not always what dancers wear onstage or in the studio.

TWO TUTUS

As women began to be cast in starring ballet roles during the nineteenth century, their costumes began to change. In 1832, Marie Taglioni appeared onstage in a gauzy white skirt, and female dancers soon started wearing similar Romantic tutus. The long net skirt of many layers hung mid-calf, showing off their feet. The famous artist Edgar Degas painted ballet dancers at the Paris Opéra in this type of skirt.

Skirts grew shorter in the late 1800s and early 1900s. Dancers started wearing what is now called a classical tutu, a stiff skirt made from ten to fifteen layers of a fabric called tulle. The short skirt sticks straight out from the hips and shows off the entire leg. Now audiences got a clear view of a dancer's technique, high jumps, and long leg extensions.

In *The Nutcracker,* the tutus of the Dew Drop Fairy and the Sugar Plum Fairy usually have thousands of shiny sequins sewn onto them by hand.

ROMANTIC TUTU

CLASSICAL TUTU

What Does a Costume Designer Do?

A costume designer researches and designs the costumes worn by dancers onstage. They must choose fabrics and styles that go with the theme, look good under bright stage lights, and are easy for dancers to spin, jump, and stretch in. They work closely with the choreographer and set designer.

IN THE STUDIO: PRACTICE CLOTHES

Most dance students wear leotards to class. Did you know the leotard was named after a person? Jules Léotard was a circus trapeze artist in the 1800s. To move better when he did his daring flips and turns (and to show off his muscular body), he designed a tight-fitting, full-body, long-sleeved suit made of a knitted jersey fabric. He called it a maillot. The name was changed to "leotard" after he died in 1870.

Dancers keep their leg muscles warm by wearing tights. Muscles stretch more easily when they're warm. A French costume designer invented tights for men so they wouldn't have to dance in heavy trousers, but women quickly put them on, too. Some dancers add wool leg warmers over their tights for extra warmth.

How do the dancers change costumes so quickly during a performance?

Dressers are positioned in the wings, the areas to the left and the right of the stage, to assist with speedy costume changes. It's dark, so they use phone flashlights to see that every hook and button is fastened. **Wardrobe coordinators** organize costumes and props neatly on racks backstage so everyone can find what they need.

FUN FACT

Ballet dancers are called "bunheads," because a dancer's hair is usually pulled away from their face into a tight bun. If long hair is left loose, a pirouetting dancer could easily end up hair-whipping a nearby dancer in the eye—or even injuring their own eyes.

In Good Company

Many dancers audition to join professional ballet companies. Once accepted, they are divided into three groups, or ranks, depending on their talent and ability.

Corps de ballet are the dancers who appear in large group numbers. These dancers must often dance in unison, doing the same move at the same time. The goal is that no single dancer stands out, which is not an easy thing to do.

Nutcracker roles: flowers, snowflakes

Soloists dance alone or with several others onstage. Soloists often understudy the principal dancers.

Nutcracker roles: Act 2 sweet treat dance

Principal dancers perform the lead roles.

Nutcracker roles: Clara, Sugar Plum Fairy, Cavalier, Nutcracker, Dew Drop Fairy, and Drosselmeyer

Mime to Me

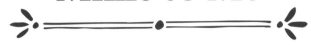

Dancers are storytellers. They communicate actions, feelings, and thoughts with their bodies. Sometimes they also use their faces and gestures to show an audience what they can't say. This kind of acting—with only facial expressions and body language—is called **mime** (short for "pantomime").

Certain mime gestures are like a special ballet sign language. Try them and see if your family or friends can guess what you're telling them.

LOOK FOR IT

Act 1 party scene, Clara mimes excitement when she gets gifts. At the beginning of Act 2, the Nutcracker Prince mimes the story of the battle with the Mouse King for the Sugar Plum Fairy.

ANGER
Bend elbows and shake your fists in the air.

SADNESS
Trace lines of tears down your cheeks.

FEAR
Hold up your hands with your palms out and lean your body back.

LOVE
Cross your hands over your heart.

REMEMBER
Touch your forehead with your index finger.

BEAUTIFUL
Make a circle around your face with the palm of your hand.

The Music

In a ballet, music is used to tell a story, create a mood, and set a tone. Listen closely to the music, and you'll be able to tell what each character is like, what they are feeling, and how they feel about other characters.

What Does a Composer Do?

A composer is a musician who writes new, original music to be performed. Composers may write the music for a full orchestra or for just one instrument. They may write a full-length ballet or a short theme for a computer game. Composers need to know about several instruments and have a "good ear" (able to hear different notes, tones, and pitches). How's your ear?

PYOTR ILYICH TCHAIKOVSKY (1840–1893)

Pyotr Ilyich Tchaikovsky was born to a wealthy family in Votkinsk, a town located in the Ural Mountains of Russia. As a boy, Tchaikovsky loved music. He played the piano every chance he got. When there wasn't a piano nearby, he'd tap out the notes on the dining table, his bed frame, a windowpane, anything nearby. When he was six years old, he once tapped a window so hard, he shattered the glass and cut his hand!

Tchaikovsky wanted to become a musician when he grew up, but his parents wouldn't allow it. They said music was not a respectable profession. At age twelve, he was sent away to boarding school to study law. He graduated and started work as a lawyer, but he hated it. He was happiest when he was playing and composing music. Finally, at age twenty-one, he quit his job.

Tchaikovsky enrolled in the new music school that had opened in St. Petersburg. At the time, the most famous composers were European. The new school wanted to train native Russians to become great composers. Tchaikovsky earned his degree and began to teach music and compose operas.

PEN PAL

As a music teacher, Tchaikovsky wasn't making a lot of money. He tried to take side jobs, but that left him with even less time to create his own music, which is what he really wanted to do. Luckily, a wealthy widow of a railway tycoon came along and decided to become his benefactor. Nadezhda von Meck so believed in his talent that, for thirteen years, she sent him money every month. This allowed him to quit his teaching job and focus solely on composing. She only had one odd rule—they could never meet in person. She feared that if she were to meet him, he wouldn't live up to how great she thought he was when she listened to his music. Instead, they sent over one thousand letters back and forth to each other.

During his lifetime, Tchaikovsky composed many operas, concertos, and great symphonies. He often combined his strict music school training with the melodies of folk songs from his childhood. He was known as a Romantic composer, because his dramatic music was filled with sweeping emotion and passion. Tchaikovsky traveled around Europe, playing his symphonies. He soon became very famous. The tsar was proud of his country's great composer and offered to pay Tchaikovsky to come home and create music only for Russia's theaters.

MUSIC TO DANCE TO

When the great Tchaikovsky agreed to team up with choreographer Marius Petipa it was a game changer for ballet. Up until then, accomplished symphony composers did not write for the ballet. Unimaginative ballet music was left to lesser composers. Tchaikovsky was the first to produce a complex, storytelling score that was exciting to listen to with or without dancers onstage. Tchaikovsky wrote the music for three of the most famous ballets: *The Sleeping Beauty, The Nutcracker,* and *Swan Lake.* Other great composers eventually followed his lead, raising the level of ballet scores.

Although he had great success and was extraordinarily popular, Tchaikovsky was often unhappy. He also tended to be a hypochondriac, convinced he was sick and going to die. Legend has it that once, while conducting, he experienced stage fright and became certain his head was about to fall off (today, this might be called a panic attack). He kept the orchestra playing, conducting with one hand and holding tight to his chin with the other. Tchaikovsky poured all his heightened emotions into his music, transforming them into melodies that were both beautiful and captivating.

In 1893, at age fifty-three, Tchaikovsky died from what's believed to have been the bacterial disease cholera. His death occurred only one year after the premiere of *The Nutcracker.*

FUN FACT

You may recognize another Tchaikovsky tune, *1812 Overture.* He wrote it to commemorate Russia's victory over Napoleon's army in 1812. It's best known for all the cannons going *BOOM!* at the end. It's often played along with Fourth of July fireworks.

THE ORCHESTRA

Sometimes when you see *The Nutcracker,* you'll hear Tchaikovsky's music played by a live orchestra. An orchestra is a large group of musicians with different instruments who play classical music together. The instruments' sounds blend to make beautiful melodies.

Orchestras are arranged in sections.

STRING SECTION

WOODWIND SECTION

BRASS SECTION

PERCUSSION SECTION

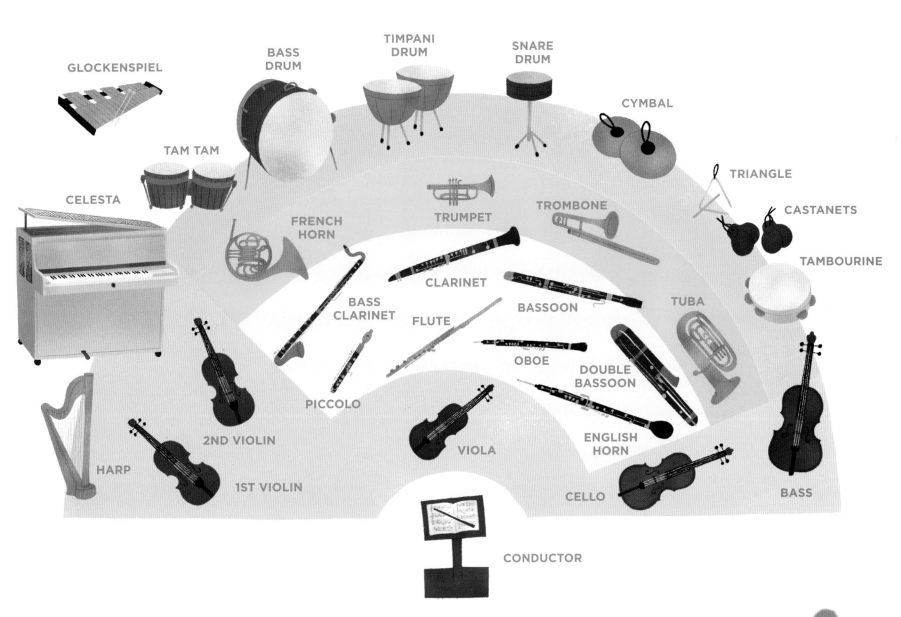

GLOCKENSPIEL

BASS DRUM

TIMPANI DRUM

SNARE DRUM

CYMBAL

TAM TAM

TRIANGLE

CELESTA

TRUMPET

TROMBONE

CASTANETS

FRENCH HORN

CLARINET

TAMBOURINE

BASS CLARINET

FLUTE

BASSOON

TUBA

HARP

PICCOLO

2ND VIOLIN

OBOE

DOUBLE BASSOON

VIOLA

ENGLISH HORN

1ST VIOLIN

CELLO

BASS

CONDUCTOR

THE ORCHESTRA PIT

The musicians sit and play in a sunken area directly in front of the stage called the **orchestra pit**. The **conductor** leads the orchestra, guiding the musicians to play at the correct times. By moving their arms or a handheld stick, called a **baton**, conductors let the musicians know when to start and stop and when to play louder or softer. The conductor stands on a raised platform so they can both watch the dancers onstage and also be seen by the musicians in the pit.

OVERTURE

At the beginning of the ballet, before the curtain goes up, the orchestra plays the **overture**. The overture's job is to set the mood, so you'll hear bits of melodies you'll recognize later in the ballet. *The Nutcracker*'s overture is bright and bouncy. The lower strings (cellos and double basses) don't play at all, only the upper strings (violins and violas).

MEET THE CELESTA

It was opening night of the first-ever production of *The Nutcracker*, and the orchestra began to play "Dance of the Sugar Plum Fairy." The audience gasped. What was that sweet, magical, bell-like sound? It came from a new instrument at the time called the **celesta**. The celesta looks like a small piano but sounds like delicate bells or a xylophone. A piano's keys/hammers hit strings, but a celesta's keys/hammers hit small metal plates. Its name comes from a French word meaning "heavenly" (just like the English word "celestial").

The instrument was invented in Paris in 1886, and Tchaikovsky discovered it in the French capital while on his way back to Russia after conducting at the opening of Carnegie Hall in New York in 1891. He secretly purchased one immediately and had it shipped to St. Petersburg. He didn't tell anyone about it or allow it to be played in rehearsals. He wanted to make sure he was the first Russian composer to use the celesta. When the orchestra played on opening night, the audience was amazed by the musical surprise.

Other composers have used the celesta. Are you a Harry Potter fan? You'll hear it in John Williams's "Hedwig's Theme" in the Harry Potter movies.

Jazz It Up

In 1960, the great American composer, pianist, and bandleader Duke Ellington and his fellow musician Billy Strayhorn transformed *The Nutcracker Suite* (the ballet's music Tchaikovsky had shortened and combined for an orchestra to play) into big-band jazz. They swapped out the flutes and strings for saxophones and muted trombones, added syncopated horns, had the drummer play standard jazz rhythms, injected both up-tempo rhythms and slow, smooth grooves, and layered in jazz harmonies. "Dance of the Reed Pipes" became "Toot Toot Tootie Toot," "March" was reimagined as "Peanut Brittle Brigade," and "Dance of the Sugar Plum Fairy" turned into the playful "Sugar Rum Cherry." Today, some versions of *The Nutcracker* use this score. Ellington and Strayhorn's jumpin' jazz makes a dancer want to twirl and swing!

Front Row: A Closer Look

The lights are going down. The orchestra is about to play the first notes of the overture. Hurry! Let the usher show you to your seat. We've saved a special one in the front row just for you. You'll have a close-up view of the cast, the sets, the costumes, and the dancers in every scene. Follow along as we spotlight the music (NOTE-WORTHY), the steps (POINTE-ERS), different staging (THIS OR THAT?), and pose interesting questions (THINK ABOUT IT). It's time to watch the show!

MEET THE CHARACTERS

Clara is the main character. (Sometimes she's named Marie or Masha.) She's a caring, independent, take-charge girl.

Fritz is Clara's energetic and mischievous younger brother.

Clara's **mother** and **father** are the hosts of the party.

DROSSELMEYER is Clara's mysterious godfather. He's a toymaker and, possibly, a magician.

The **party guests** and their **CHILDREN** enjoy the festivities and dance.

COLUMBINE and **HARLEQUIN** are life-size mechanical dolls that magically come to life to entertain the party guests. They're both characters borrowed from a traditional form of Italian theater called commedia dell'arte.

The **NUTCRACKER** is Clara's wooden toy that becomes a charming prince. In the original story, he is also Drosselmeyer's nephew, who has been transformed into a wooden doll by the Mouse King.

The **toy soldiers** are part of the Nutcracker's army.

The **Mouse King** is the mouse leader. In some productions, the Mouse King has one head, and in others, seven!

The **mice** are part of the Mouse King's army.

The **SNOWFLAKES** swirl together into a dancing blizzard.

The **Sugar Plum Fairy** is the ruler of the Land of Sweets.

Chocolate performs a Spanish-inspired dance.

COFFEE performs a Middle Eastern–inspired dance.

Tea performs a Chinese-inspired dance.

Mirliton or the **marzipan shepherdesses** perform a dance with reed pipes.

The **CANDY CANES** or **TREPAK DANCERS** perform a Russian-inspired dance, sometimes with hoops.

Mother Ginger is a large woman hiding her children under her enormous skirt.

The **polichinelles** are Mother Ginger's dancing children.

The **Dew Drop Fairy** waltzes with the flowers and is second in importance, after the Sugar Plum Fairy, in the Land of Sweets.

The **FLOWERS** all waltz together.

The **Cavalier** is the Sugar Plum Fairy's dashing dance partner.

Some Nutty Questions

What's a nutcracker?

Exactly what it sounds like—a tool used to crack the hard shell of a nut. Decorative wooden nutcrackers were first made in Germany in the late 1700s. One story says the first was carved by a puppet-maker. Nutcrackers were often painted to look like kings, soldiers, and police officers.

Why were kids given nutcracker dolls at Christmastime?

Bowls of nuts were traditionally placed on holiday celebration tables. According to old German legends, a nutcracker brings good luck, and their powerful nut-cracking jaws ward away evil spirits. Sounds like a good gift— practical and magical!

The Party

The ballet opens with a big Christmas Eve party at Clara's home. Her younger brother, Fritz, runs about mischievously with the other boys, while Clara talks excitedly with her friends, and the adults dance together. The mysterious toymaker Drosselmeyer arrives with two large presents. The boxes are opened, and Harlequin and Columbine step out. He winds up the life-sized dolls, and they magically dance!

NOTE-WORTHY ♫

- "March" is the happy piece of music heard at the beginning of the party scene. Tchaikovsky used small cymbals and drums to make the music fun and festive.
- The music darkens to announce the arrival of the mysterious Drosselmeyer. We hear tubas, trombones, and a horn.

POINTE-ERS 🩰

- The children dance with a lot of traveling steps, skips, and jumps. They do a Gallop, a popular dance during Victorian times named after the fast gait of a horse.
- Columbine and Harlequin dance with stiff, jerky steps to show they are mechanical dolls.

THINK ABOUT IT 💡

Because the ballet was written long ago, the party children in most productions are instructed to act and mime according to traditional gender stereotypes. The boys are naughty and play with toy soldiers, while the girls are sweet and play with dolls. But girls can also be naughty and boys are also sweet—and kids play with all different kinds of toys. If you were choreographing the ballet, what would you have the kids in the party scene do?

The Nutcracker

Drosselmeyer has brought his goddaughter, Clara, the most special gift of all—a wooden nutcracker. Jealous Fritz grabs for it. Clara holds on. They both pull, and the nutcracker's jaw cracks. Clara's in tears until Drosselmeyer bandages the doll. The dancing continues, then the guests say their good-byes, and it is time for bed. Clara places the nutcracker gently under the Christmas tree.

NOTE-WORTHY ♫

- The orchestra uses a rattle for the sound of the nutcracker cracking nuts.
- The parents' last dance is known as the "Grandfather Dance." The music is a German folk tune traditionally played at the end of a party to signal it was time for everyone to go home.

POINTE-ERS 🩰

The adults dance a traditional ballroom waltz with *balancé*, a rocking step where the weight shifts from one foot to the other.

The Tree Grows

Clara sneaks out of bed and back downstairs to check on her broken toy. With the nutcracker cradled in her arms, she falls asleep. As the clock strikes midnight, the Christmas tree grows and grows—and the real world transforms into a fantasy world.

NOTE-WORTHY ♫

- As the tree grows, the string instruments play a series of rising scales (four notes up, two notes down, four notes up, two down, etc.) in a melody that crescendos, or grows ever louder.
- A crashing cymbal is usually used for the clock chiming midnight.

The Mice Battle

Clara's nutcracker and her brother's toy soldiers magically come to life. Enormous mice scamper about, led by the Mouse King. They attack the soldiers—it's a battle! The Mouse King and the Nutcracker fight a tense duel. Just when it looks like the Nutcracker will lose, Clara throws her slipper at the Mouse King and he drops to the floor! His mouse army carries his lifeless body offstage.

NOTE-WORTHY ♫

The music in the battle scene features higher notes for the soldiers versus lower notes for the mice, and it was composed to sound like a battle. As the battle heats up, the music grows faster and louder.

POINTE-ERS 🩰

- The soldiers march stiffly in straight lines with straight bodies and step together as a large group. The frisky mice dart and weave about the stage in small groups.
- Like in a real battle, the two opposing armies face each other. One charges forward, then the other charges, and the two sides take turns going back and forth.

THINK ABOUT IT 💡

When E. T. A. Hoffmann wrote his story, machines were just being introduced to do work previously done by hand. But many people were unsure of and frightened by the new machines. A few even wondered if they moved by magic. When you watch the ballet, can you see this uncertainty portrayed in the partygoers' reaction to Drosselmeyer, and when the toy soldiers come to life?

THIS OR THAT? ✦

In some productions, you'll see mice, and in others, you'll see rats.

Land of Snow

The Nutcracker has transformed into a dashing prince! Clara and her Nutcracker Prince travel through a wintery forest of firs in the Land of Snow. The snow falls gently at first, but soon Clara and the prince are caught up in an enchanted blizzard.

NOTE-WORTHY ♫

- As Clara and the prince enter the Land of Snow, the flutes and piccolos play quick three-note patterns to sound like tiny snow flurries. As the snow turns into a storm, other instruments join in, and the music grows ever faster and louder.
- Two harps play arpeggios. In an arpeggio, the notes of a chord are played one note at a time.

POINTE-ERS

The snowflakes dance in formation, doing steps at the exact same time. They twirl in sync to create the wondrous effect of a snowstorm. The dancers' arms mimic the shape of a snowflake. A lot of stamina, or energy, is needed for this dance.

THIS OR THAT?

In some productions, a shimmering Snow Queen and Snow King lead the dancing snowflakes.

THINK ABOUT IT

Snow is water vapor from a cloud that freezes into tiny ice crystals. The air needs to be cold for precipitation to become snow (and not rain). But if a theater pumped in freezing air, dancers would be pirouetting in puffer coats. So how do **set designers** make it snow? Paper! Thousands of snowflakes are cut out of flame-retardant paper (so they don't catch fire under hot stage lights) and sprinkled onto the stage from above. Huge fans blow them about to create a blizzard. While it's fun to catch fresh snow on your tongue, the dancers know to keep their mouths shut tight. The paper snowflakes taste terrible!

Land of Sweets

Clara and her prince leave the snowstorm and enter the Land of Sweets, where everything is spun from sugar. They are greeted by its ruler, the Sugar Plum Fairy, who is told about the defeat of the Mouse King. As a reward for their bravery, she invites them to sit upon a majestic throne and watch a pageant of delicious, dancing sweets.

POINTE-ERS

The Nutcracker is a story ballet, but in Act 2, the story takes a long pause while the sweet treats do five short dances to entertain Clara and the prince. These dances are called **divertissements**.

FUN FACT

The "Arabian" coffee song was meant to sound Middle Eastern but is based on an Eastern European lullaby traditionally sung to sick children.

THINK ABOUT IT 💡

Each divertissement celebrates a sweet from a different part of the world. However, the original choreographers and costume designers hadn't visited many of these places and didn't properly research them. Instead, they created steps and costumes based on racially insensitive and insulting stereotypes that were common at that time. This was especially true with the dances and costumes of Coffee and Tea. Although the dance world was slow to correct this, many companies have made significant changes to these divertissements and are now using more accurate costumes and movements to celebrate Middle Eastern and Chinese cultures.

NOTE-WORTHY 🎵

Listen for . . .

- Chocolate—the trumpet solo and the snap of Spanish castanets
- Coffee—the repeating rhythm of the cellos and basses behind the oboes' and violins' melody
- Tea—the high notes of the flutes, piccolos, and violins and the low notes of the bassoons and double basses
- Candy Canes or Trepak—the energetic melody that grows ever faster, played by all the instruments
- Mirlitons/Marzipan/Shepherdess— the trio of flutes carrying the playful melody

THIS OR THAT? ✦

The fifth divertissement goes by different names in different productions. It may be Mirliton, Marzipan, Dance of the Reed Pipes or Flutes, or Dance of the Shepherdess.

What's a mirliton?

A mirliton is a reed pipe, which is a flute-like instrument that makes a sound similar to a kazoo. Mirliton is also a small sweet French pastry that's rolled into a tube, like a pipe or flute, and filled with chocolate mousse or marzipan.

What's marzipan?

It's a candy made from ground almonds and sugar that's formed into a thick paste and then shaped into cute fruits, animals, or people. It's a popular Christmas treat in Europe.

Why are there sometimes shepherdesses?

In folklore, a shepherdess would play a reed pipe to her flock of sheep.

BIG MAMA

Larger-than-life, spirited Mother Ginger glides onto the stage and—*surprise!*—out pop little polichinelles (clown-children) from beneath her enormous hoop skirt. And here's a secret: Mother Ginger is often played by a male dancer dressed as a woman. He balances on stilts or a rolling cart, with room for many dancers hiding under the heavy skirt.

The character of Mother Ginger is thought to be inspired a famous nursery rhyme. Do you know which one?

*There was an old woman
who lived in a shoe.
She had so many children,
she didn't know what to do.*

For the child performers in the ballet, the polichinelles dance is the most technically demanding. They must mirror one another and dance in couples to the bouncy music.

Waltz of the Flowers

Pretty sugar flowers turn their faces to the sun and open their petals. They twirl in mesmerizing patterns, led by the delicate Dew Drop Fairy. The enchanted pixie flutters and flies through the air, as if being carried by a sweet breeze.

NOTE-WORTHY ♫

- The music starts with a harp solo. Then the horns and clarinet join in. The woodwinds' melody is meant to sound like a gentle breeze blowing through the flowers.
- The music is a waltz, which has a one-two-three beat. There is one strong beat ("um") and two weaker beats ("pa pa").

POINTE-ERS 🩰

- The dancing flowers waltz about the stage with graceful, sweeping motions.
- In the Balanchine version, the Dew Drop Fairy's entrance on a diagonal sometimes features fouettés, or whipping turns. The quick turns and fast footwork in her solo make it look as if her feet have wings, never touching the floor.

The Sugar Plum Fairy

After the Sweets dance, the glittering Sugar Plum Fairy and her Cavalier take center stage. They perform the most famous dance in the ballet, the grand pas de deux. They dance together, then he dances alone, followed by her solo, "Dance of the Sugar Plum Fairy." At the end, they dance together again.

NOTE-WORTHY 🎵

- For the Sugar Plum Fairy's dance, Petipa asked Tchaikovsky to write music that "sounded like drops of water splashing in a fountain." Tchaikovsky used the new instrument, the celesta, to achieve this delicate sound.

- The Sugar Plum Fairy music has the strings playing many slow, descending scales. There's a story that Tchaikovsky's friend bet him that he couldn't write a melody made up only of notes in a scale. Guess what? Tchaikovsky did it and won the bet!

POINTE-ERS 🩰

- A **pas de deux** is a romantic dance, usually danced by the two best dancers in the ballet. Pas de deux means "step of two" or "dance for two." A classical or traditional pas de deux has four sections—section one is a **duet** that starts slowly; section two is the man's solo, also called a **variation**, followed by section three, the woman's solo. Then comes the final section, called the **coda**, where the dancers usually perform a series of impressive steps that end with an exciting flourish.

• There's a lot of difficult pointe work, high acrobatic lifts, and dangerous catches in the pas de deux.

THIS OR THAT? ⊕
Some productions replace the Sugar Plum Fairy with Clara as a grown-up princess and the Cavalier with her Nutcracker Prince.

What's a Sugar Plum?
It's a round Christmas candy that was popular in Europe from the 1500s through the 1800s. But here's the confusing thing—there were no plums in sugar plums! Instead, a seed, nut, or piece of spice was covered in a hard sugar shell (very much like an M&M).

What's a Cavalier?
Cavalier is a classical ballet term for the male partner of a female dancer. In the original *Nutcracker,* the Cavalier's name was Prince Coqueluche, which means "whooping cough" in French. Weird, right? But he wasn't named after a virus. He was probably named for a sore-throat lozenge. Okay, also weird, but back then cough drops were sweet like candy! Balanchine renamed him Cavalier.

FUN FACT
The Sugar Plum Fairy's tutu at the Oregon Ballet Theatre was made from twelve layers of tulle. If all that tulle was unrolled and lined up end-to-end, it would stretch the length of about 1⅓ football fields!

The Good-bye

Clara and the Nutcracker Prince lead everyone in a final dance and then say good-bye to the Land of Sweets.

NOTE-WORTHY ♫

The last piece of music is called "Final Waltz and Apotheosis." In music, an apotheosis is a big, grand finale. Listen closely and you'll hear the melody that began Act 2 repeat in the final waltz, and the celesta and the harp ring out again in the apotheosis. The whole orchestra, led by the strings, comes together for the loud and dramatic finish.

THIS OR THAT? ✛

In some productions, Clara returns safely back home to the sofa where she'd fallen asleep the night before. Sometimes she gets there on a flying sleigh pulled by reindeer. In other productions, Clara and the Nutcracker Prince continue together on their journey to lands unknown.

Mixed Nuts!

No production of *The Nutcracker* is completely faithful to the original, so no one "true" *Nutcracker* exists. While some revisions and changes have been small, others have flipped the holiday ballet upside down on its wooden head. Every year, roughly one thousand different productions of *The Nutcracker* are performed throughout the world. Since there's not nearly enough space in this book to describe all of them, here's a handful of some not-so-traditional "nuts."

THE HARD NUT from contemporary choreographer MARK MORRIS places the story in a 1970s American rec room. In the first act, the partygoers wear bell-bottoms and plaid leisure suits, an army of GI Joe toys fight the rats, and both men and women dance on pointe as snowflakes, wearing tutus. Act 2 includes a story within Hoffmann's original tale called "The Story of the Hard Nut," which wasn't used in the original ballet. It explains how the prince turned into a nutcracker.

Three funny rats narrate DEBBIE ALLEN's *HOT CHOCOLATE NUTCRACKER*, a modernized retelling, in which dancers perform a mix of ballet, modern, jazz, tap, hip-hop, and flamenco. They also bring Bollywood to Act 2 with a spirited Bharatanatyam-style dance from India. Original compositions from artists such as Mariah Carey replace Tchaikovsky's score.

The **Pacific Northwest Ballet** enjoys collaborating with famous children's book authors and illustrators. Both Maurice Sendak (*Where the Wild Things Are*) and Ian Falconer (the Olivia series) have designed extravagant sets and costumes for productions.

Canada's **Royal Winnipeg Ballet**'s *Nutcracker* features a scene with a hockey game!

The **Joffrey Ballet** set their production at the 1893 World's Fair in Chicago.

In the **Washington Ballet**'s Revolutionary War–themed *Nutcracker,* the Nutcracker is George Washington, the Mouse King is Britain's King George III, and Mother Ginger's huge skirt is a carousel!

The **National Ballet of China**'s Spring Festival–themed *Nutcracker* features Yuanyuan (Clara), sword-bearing tigers, the twelve animals of the Chinese zodiac, and a Crane Goddess instead of the Sugar Plum Fairy.

MATTHEW BOURNE's *NUTCRACKER!* features Clara as an orphan who lives in the ramshackle Dr. Dross's Orphanage for Waifs and Strays. She goes on a dream adventure to an over-the-top, neon-infused world.

The **Dutch National Ballet**'s *Nutcracker* takes place in Amsterdam in 1810, during the Dutch feast of Sinterklaas. And Act 2 happens inside a magic lantern!

The **Australian Ballet**'s production, choreographed by Peter Wright, had a fifteen-year-old Clara transported to the Land of Sweets on a flying goose!

South Africa's **Joburg Ballet** swapped out the snow for sun, sand, and baobab trees (Christmas comes during the summer in the southern hemisphere). Clara is led by a *sangoma*, or ancient healer, through the Kalahari Desert, where ancient Bushmen cave paintings come to life.

THE HARLEM NUTCRACKER featured Clara as a widowed grandmother. The party scene replaced European dances with the neighbors doing the salsa and a gospel choir. Act 2 included Clara visiting Club Sweets in the Harlem Renaissance. Many of the variations in the second act used the jazzy tunes of Duke Ellington and Billy Strayhorn.

EASTERN CONNECTICUT BALLET's *NUTCRACKER* takes place in an 1850s New England whaling village. Clara's father is a sea captain, the tree turns into a giant boat, and there are pirate rats and a magical seaport.

Tony Williams's high-energy, multicultural **Urban Nutcracker** blends the music of Tchaikovsky and Ellington. Set in present-day multicultural Boston, Clarice is swept into a fantasy world of tap, hip-hop, flamenco, and jazz.

Festival Ballet Albuquerque's *The Nutcracker in the Land of Enchantment* celebrates southwestern heritage with a lively fandango, snakes, and a Cochiti Pueblo storyteller doll.

New Ballet Ensemble's *Nut Remix* sets the ballet in a café on Memphis's Beale Street and mixes in African dance, flamenco, and hip-hop, along with live flamenco guitarists and West African drummers.

THE HIP HOP NUTCRACKER showcases supercharged break dancing to Tchaikovsky tunes spun by a DJ.

Ballet Superstitions

Dancers can be very superstitious, and many dancers perform quirky rituals before the curtain rises to guarantee a good show. Some do their stretches in the same order every time. Some eat a peanut-butter-and-banana sandwich before putting on their costume. Here are some other well-known dance superstitions:

It's bad luck to give dancers flowers *before* they go onstage.

It's bad luck for a dancer to look directly at the audience from backstage or the wings.

If a dancer drops or spills makeup powder, they must dance in it or they'll have bad luck.

Whistling backstage jinxes the performance.

Knitting, onstage or backstage, will bring bad luck.

If a cat walks across the stage during rehearsal, something bad will happen in the show.

A bad dress rehearsal means the show will be a hit.

Never wish dancers "good luck," or you'll jinx them. And although people say "break a leg" to actors, no dancer wants *that* to happen! So, instead, dancers say *Merde!* to one another. Merde is a not-nice way to say horse manure . . . or poop. The superstition supposedly started in the 1800s, when wealthy audiences for the Paris Opera Ballet arrived at the theater in horse-drawn carriages. If the show was sold out, there'd be a lot of horses out front—and big piles of manure. The more manure, the more popular the ballet. Saying *merde* to a dancer was like saying, "There's a whole lot of folks out there watching you, so good luck!" The correct response is *oui* ("yes" in French). Saying *thank you* reverses all the good luck.

Nutcracker Star Power

Every professional ballet dancer has a memory (or two or three) of dancing in the famous holiday ballet. Many performed for the very first time onstage as party children or polichinelles. Some were chosen to dance the role of Clara, but many principals tell stories of auditioning for Clara and *not* getting the role. Nevertheless, they still went on to ballet greatness. All dancers agree that being part of such a big and joyous production was an important (and fun!) part of their dance education.

The list of amazing, iconic dancers who've delighted audiences over the years in *The Nutcracker* goes on and on. It's extremely difficult to choose only a few to highlight. Here are a handful of greats who've jetéd over obstacles and broken new ground.

NUTCRACKER ★ POWER

MARIA TALLCHIEF
(1925–2013)

SUGAR PLUM FAIRY

"If anything at all, perfection is not when there is nothing to add, but when there is nothing left to take away."

ELIZABETH MARIE TALL CHIEF was born in Fairfax, Oklahoma. Her father was a member of the Osage Nation, and her mother was Scotch-Irish-Dutch. For hundreds of years, the Osage populated the central U.S. plains, but in the 1800s, white settlers forced them onto reservations, so they could farm and build on their land. Maria lived on the Osage reservation, but when she turned eight, her family moved to Los Angeles, California. Here the kids in school teased her about her Native heritage. She changed the spelling of her last name to one word so they wouldn't be so cruel, but it didn't help much.

Maria started studying ballet seriously at age twelve with the famous Russian dancer and choreographer Bronislava Nijinska. Madame Nijinska would say, "When you sleep, sleep like ballerina. Even on street waiting for bus, stand like ballerina." Maria began to live and breathe ballet. As soon as she graduated high school, Maria took a train to New York City to audition for the Ballets Russes de Monte-Carlo. At first, they didn't accept her. But when another dancer abruptly left, Maria was invited on their tour—leaving right away! She had to learn all the steps in just a few days. Because all the other dancers were Russian (and to hide her heritage), the director asked her to change her Osage last name to Tallchieva. Maria remembered the hurt she'd felt at school. This time she refused to change her name to fit in. She was proud to be an Osage.

Maria was in the corps de ballet but was also chosen to understudy the lead. The other dancers said she was too young and inexperienced for this honor, and silently Maria agreed. One day, when the lead couldn't go on, Maria was thrust into the spotlight . . . and she was spectacular! She soon became the featured soloist. The company's new choreographer, a young George Balanchine, tutored her, changing her technique, fixing the arch of her foot, and elongating her neck and arms. Balanchine made several of his famous ballets for her, and the two were married for a brief time.

In 1947, Maria Tallchief became the first Native principal dancer at the New York City Ballet. In 1954, Balanchine cast Maria as the Sugar Plum Fairy in *The Nutcracker*. Her graceful, emotional performance was part of what made the unknown production into a success.

Maria went on to dance around the world, and after retiring in 1965, she founded the Chicago City Ballet. She never forgot her Osage heritage and spoke out against injustices and discrimination, famously declaring, "I wanted to be appreciated as a prima ballerina who happened to be a Native American, never as someone who was an American Indian ballerina."

ALICIA ALONSO
(1920-2019)

SUGAR PLUM FAIRY

"A dancer should learn from all the arts. Go to museums and look at the paintings. See how they balance things. Everything you do in the arts enriches you."

Born in Havana, Cuba, **ALICIA ERNESTINA DE LA CARIDAD DEL COBRE MARTÍNEZ DEL HOYO** always knew she'd grow up to be a ballet dancer. Her first professional teacher was a Russian dancer who'd stayed behind in Havana after his company's tour. Because it was the Depression and money was tight, there weren't any pointe shoes on the island. One day a man who'd gotten a pair as a gift in Italy brought them to the school. Like in the Cinderella fairy tale, only one student's feet fit into the shoes. It was Alicia!

At age sixteen, she married Fernando Alonso, a fellow student, and moved with him to New York. Her first dancing job was in a chorus line in a Broadway show, and then she was made a soloist for the American Ballet Caravan, which later became the New York City Ballet. In 1941, Alicia became one of the first members of the American Ballet Theater. That same year, when she was just nineteen, Alicia started bumping into things. Something was wrong with her vision.

Doctors discovered she had a detached retina. Alicia went through three painful surgeries and was put on total bed rest. Her eyes were bandaged, and she was forbidden to laugh, cry, shake her head, or even move her body (although she did stretch and point her feet!). Fernando sat by her side every day, and he taught her the great roles of classical ballet by using their fingers. She recalled, "I danced in my mind. Blinded, motionless, flat on my back."

She was partially blind, and her doctor warned that if she tried to dance, she'd go fully blind. Alicia insisted upon dancing. In 1943, she was asked to fill in for the American Ballet Theater's injured lead dancer in *Giselle,* one of the ballets she'd memorized while in bed. Alicia brought the house down! She also starred in *Swan Lake* and other difficult ballets. Despite not being able to see, Alicia was technically flawless and danced with immense passion.

Her partners were all trained to be exactly where she needed them, since she could only see shadows. They'd also whisper instructions. Strong spotlights in different colors were placed around the stage to help guide her.

In 1948, she returned to Cuba to start the Alicia Alonso Ballet Company, which is now called Ballet Nacional de Cuba. She continued to guest star around the world. When Ballets Russes de Monte-Carlo performed selected excerpts from *The Nutcracker* at the Metropolitan Opera House in New York in 1957, Alicia danced the Sugar Plum Fairy. Alicia remained the artistic director and choreographer of the Ballet Nacional de Cuba until her death at age ninety-eight.

MIKHAIL BARYSHNIKOV
(1948-)

NUTCRACKER PRINCE

"I do not try to dance better than anyone else. I only try to dance better than myself."

MIKHAIL BARYSHNIKOV was born in Riga, Latvia, then part of the Communist Soviet Union (USSR). His strict father was a military officer, and his mother worked in a clothing shop. She liked ballet, and when he was nine, she enrolled Misha (as he is known) in classes. Misha channeled all his energy into dance and moved on to the famous Vaganova ballet school in St. Petersburg (then known as Leningrad). He spent hours in the studio practicing each step and body position. He wanted to be the best, but he was worried. He was the shortest in his class. He was told he was too short to be a top dancer. Every night, Misha slept on a hard wooden plank, hoping it would help him grow faster. (It didn't.)

His amazing skill, athleticism, and artistic expression landed him a soloist spot at the Mariinsky Ballet (also called the Kirov Ballet). He danced to great acclaim throughout the USSR. But because he was shorter than many of the female dancers (he only grew to five foot seven), he wasn't given certain lead parts. This frustrated him. He was also frustrated by the government's strict control over his life and his dancing. While on tour to different Western countries, he'd seen the creative freedom and the opportunities available there. But defection (fleeing the country) was a crime in the Soviet Union. If caught, the defector and his family would be punished and possibly killed. Misha felt he had no other choice: "I was at the peak of my career. Time was running out. The creative mood of ballet was depressing. I was not free to fly, in every sense." He took a bold leap. After a performance in Canada, he went out the stage door and started running. His fans, eager for autographs, chased him, thinking it was a game. But Misha spotted the Soviet police nearby, watching him. He raced into a getaway car sent by his friends and sped off to safety before they could grab him.

Misha moved to the United States and quickly became the dazzling star of the American Ballet Theater. In 1977, *The Nutcracker* was the first full-length piece he choreographed. It became a famous made-for-television movie, starring Gelsey Kirkland as Clara and himself as the Nutcracker Prince. On-screen, Misha showed off split leaps and dizzying pirouettes. He changed up the story, having Clara and the Nutcracker Prince dance the final pas de deux.

Misha later joined the New York City Ballet, where he worked with George Balanchine. He became the artistic director of the American Ballet Theater, acted in several Hollywood movies, became a modern dancer, founded the White Oak Dance Project with Mark Morris, and now directs the Baryshnikov Arts Center, which he founded as a gathering place for artists of all kinds.

CARLOS ACOSTA
(1973-)

NUTCRACKER PRINCE

"Allow yourself the freedom to commit mistakes. You're always learning, so be curious."

CARLOS ACOSTA

has lived a true rags-to-riches fairy tale. Born in Havana, Cuba, Carlos was the youngest of eleven children. His father was a truck driver, his mother was often ill, and the family was extremely poor. His mother once had to cook their pet rabbits because she had nothing else for the kids to eat. Carlos ran wild, skipping school and break-dancing in the streets. His father was worried about him and told Carlos he had to audition for ballet school. There, he hoped his son would get the discipline he needed—plus they gave out free lunches.

Carlos had never seen a ballet, so for his audition he break-danced. The teachers were shocked! But they recognized his natural talent and flexibility and signed him up. Carlos hated ballet school (he wanted to play soccer) and behaved very badly. He was kicked out, but his father managed to get him into a different ballet school. While on a school trip to Ballet Nacional de Cuba, Carlos's attitude changed. "I saw a dancer called Alberto Terrero," he recalled. "I was astonished with his jumps, and I decided I wanted to emulate him. From that day on, ballet began to grow inside of me."

He started to train seriously. "My route to ballet has always been to be the hardest worker. First to the class, last to leave," he said. And at age sixteen, he started winning important international ballet competitions. Two years later, he joined the English National Ballet as their youngest principal dancer. England was cold and gray, and Carlos desperately missed his home and family. When he suffered a bad ankle injury and needed surgery, Carlos decided to return to sunny Cuba.

But he was soon back at the barre, this time dancing with the Ballet Nacional de Cuba under the company's founder, Alicia Alonso. Because of Cuba's Communist government, he earned the equivalent of only one dollar a month. When the Houston Ballet invited him to join and offered to pay him a lot more, Carlos agreed. He made his American stage debut as the Nutcracker Prince in *The Nutcracker*. Several years later he moved to London to join the Royal Ballet, becoming their first Black principal dancer and a major star. With his legendary high jumps and powerful leaps, he delighted new audiences once again as the Nutcracker Prince. Carlos had incredible charisma and a dynamic stage presence in addition to talent and skill. He's considered one of the best dancers of all time. Carlos founded his own dance company in Cuba, Acosta Danza, and is the director of the Birmingham Royal Ballet.

YUAN YUAN TAN
(1977-)

SUGAR PLUM FAIRY, SNOW QUEEN

"My Chinese side comes out in my dancing. There's a certain in-the-moment sentimentality, an appreciation for the smallest details."

YUAN YUAN TAN became a ballet star because of a flip of a coin. Born in Shanghai, China, Yuan Yuan liked to dance but never had big tutu-wearing dreams. When she was ten, she was asked to join the Shanghai Ballet School. Her father refused. He worried about injuries and a short career. He believed she should stay in "regular" school and study to become a doctor. But Yuan Yuan's mother, who'd always wished to be a dancer herself, wanted her daughter to do ballet. So how did her parents decide? They flipped a coin—and ballet won the toss!

Yuan Yuan started at the ballet school at age eleven, and at first, she hid in the corner during class. The other kids had been dancing for years. "It was hard to see all the girls do things that I couldn't," she said. But she built up her skill and her confidence. Soon she was the best in the class. At age fourteen, she won first place in an international ballet competition in Paris. The artistic director for the San Francisco Ballet invited her to join the company once her training was complete. In 1995, at only seventeen, Yuan Yuan bypassed the entry-level corps de ballet contract, or position, to become the youngest soloist in the company's history and also the first Chinese soloist.

The move to San Francisco was difficult. Yuan Yuan didn't speak English, and the style of dancing, especially all the Balanchine choreography, was different from how she'd been trained. But once again, she worked tirelessly. Whenever she wanted to quit, she reminded herself of the coin toss and the way ballet had chosen *her.* Two years later, she was promoted to principal dancer, becoming the youngest principal dancer in the history of the San Francisco Ballet and the first Chinese dancer to reach that rank in a major company.

YY (as she's known) has danced the roles of the Sugar Plum Fairy and the Snow Queen and appeared in *The Nutcracker* on PBS's *Great Performances.* She's considered one of the most talented dancers from China and was named a Hero of Asia in the Asian edition of *Time* magazine. Yuan Yuan astounds audiences with her grace and stamina. She's been a principal dancer for longer than any dancer in the history of the San Francisco Ballet. And do you want to know a secret? Yuan Yuan says she still gets nervous before going onstage!

PALOMA HERRERA
(1975-)

CLARA, SUGAR PLUM FAIRY, SNOW QUEEN

"It's not enough to just be special and have the attention . . . You have to really love what you do and always want to make it better."

PALOMA HERRERA was always sure of one thing—she *loved* to dance. She also loved pink satin pointe shoes. It was the pointe shoes that first captured her interest as a tiny girl. Born in Buenos Aires, Argentina, Paloma began studying ballet at age seven with the great Olga Ferri. Extremely talented, she soon won several major competitions in South America. When Paloma was eleven, her family sent her to the former Soviet Union to study at the Minsk Ballet School. She then studied in London and, at age fifteen, joined New York's School of American Ballet. She arrived in the city not knowing English and had to live with family friends. But Paloma was a quick study, and after just sixth months, she was chosen to dance the lead role in *Raymonda* (also choreographed by Marius Petipa). She joined American Ballet Theater's corps de ballet in 1991, was promoted to soloist two years later, and just two years after that, at the age of nineteen, became the youngest person in the company's history to be made principal dancer.

Paloma traveled the world, dancing triumphantly on every major ballet stage. She inspired thousands of young dancers with her grace and power. Unlike many willowy dancers, Paloma proudly displayed her muscles and incredible strength in her performances. She danced many roles in *The Nutcracker* and has said, "*Nutcracker* is a ballet that I love dancing. The music is just incredible." Paloma threw herself into every role she danced, always working to become even better than she already was. She once said, "Every time I leave the stage after a performance, I want to get back out there and do it again, because I have just learned in that last performance how to improve it." After twenty-four years with the American Ballet Theater, Paloma retired in 2015 and became director of the Ballet Estable del Teatro Colón in Buenos Aires, Argentina.

MISTY COPELAND
(1982-)

CLARA, SUGAR PLUM FAIRY, COLUMBINE, SPANISH DANCER

"Other people's words are very powerful . . . You can't let them define you. Take what you think is going to help you and don't let it beat you down."

An "unlikely ballerina" is how **MISTY COPELAND** describes herself. Born in Kansas City, Missouri, Misty moved to San Pedro, California, at age two. Her entire family—her single mom, Misty herself, and her five brothers and sisters—all lived in one run-down motel room. Misty often had to sleep on the floor. Her mom worked many jobs to feed them all. One day, when Misty was thirteen, her older sister convinced her to try out for the middle school drill team. After the audition, the coach called. Misty was officially on the team—*and* the coach made her captain of the sixty-girl squad! She also suggested Misty try the free ballet class at the local Boys & Girls Club.

Misty sat on the sidelines wearing her gym clothes and socks, too shy and scared to join in the ballet class. After two weeks of Misty watching, the teacher encouraged her to try. Misty was a natural! The teacher said that Misty could be a *great* ballet dancer if she had the proper training. "It was the first time I ever felt beautiful," Misty said. "[Ballet] gave me a voice without having to speak, and I'd never had that before."

Misty took ballet classes five days a week and, in just three months, was lacing up toe shoes! After dancing for only eight months, she took on her first stage role as Clara in *The Nutcracker.* Many years later, Misty said, "It was the first ballet I ever saw, it was the first ballet I ever danced in. I've literally played every role, but I would definitely say Clara is my favorite." The next year, she danced the Sugar Plum Fairy. The year after that, she performed in Debbie Allen's *Hot Chocolate Nutcracker.*

Misty wanted to go to a dance academy but received only rejection letters. She was told her body was wrong for ballet. She was too muscular, too short, and too curvy. What wasn't said—and what Misty knew they meant—was that she was Black. The dancers at all the top companies were mostly white with tall, thin bodies. Misty didn't look like them. She worked extremely hard, and she was determined to prove the academies wrong. She won several major competitions and was chosen for the summer intensive program at the American Ballet Theater (ABT), eventually performing with their second company. After high school, Misty was invited to join ABT's corps de ballet. As the only Black dancer in the company, she often felt very alone. But she continued to do what she loved passionately—dance.

At age twenty-four, Misty Copeland was made the first Black soloist at ABT. But just as people were exclaiming how amazing she was as the lead in Igor Stravinsky's *Firebird,* she suffered a major back injury. Many said that was the end of her dance career. Like before, Misty proved them wrong. After surgery, she returned to the stage better than ever. In 2015, she made history again, becoming the first Black principal dancer in ABT's seventy-six-year history.

Misty has continued to break down barriers to shine as one of ballet's brightest stars. In addition to being named one of the one hundred most influential people in the world by *Time* magazine, Misty has excelled as an author, a Broadway performer, and a film star in Disney's *The Nutcracker and the Four Realms*. Not bad for a shy girl with an unconventional body who took her first ballet lesson at age thirteen!

TILER PECK
(1989-)

SUGAR PLUM FAIRY, DEW DROP FAIRY, MARZIPAN

"Growing up in the dance world, you can easily get caught up comparing yourself to other ballerinas . . . You don't have to be perfect. You have to be able to own your uniqueness and use it to make you the best version of yourself."

TILER PECK was born with dance shoes on. While other toddlers were playing in sandboxes, two-year-old Tiler was taking lessons at her mom's Bakersfield, California, ballet studio. By age six, she was training in ballet, jazz, and hip-hop four days a week. Her rise into the spotlight was lightning-fast. She made her professional Broadway debut playing Gracie Shinn in *The Music Man* when she was only eleven. At that point, Tiler's main focus was on jazz. She didn't really like ballet, even though her mom was a ballet teacher. Ballet was difficult, took a lot of concentration, and wasn't nearly as much fun as dancing to a pop song. That all changed one night in New York City.

Tiler's family took her to see *George Balanchine's The Nutcracker*. Tiler was on the edge of her seat for the entire performance. As the curtain closed, Tiler turned to her dad and announced that someday he'd be watching *her* on that very stage dancing the role of the Sugar Plum Fairy. Tiler began to take classes at the School of American Ballet and found she really enjoyed Balanchine's jazzy style of ballet. When she was fifteen, she was invited to join New York City Ballet's corps de ballet. She was quickly promoted to soloist and made principal dancer when she was only twenty. Tiler went on to dance the leading roles in hundreds of ballets. She also danced on Broadway, starring in the musical *On the Town*. Although she'd danced Dew Drop in earlier productions, Tiler was overcome with emotion when she was cast as the Sugar Plum Fairy in 2017. This role had made her want to be a ballet dancer! She said, "It felt sort of like a dream, because it is the role that every ballerina wants and hopes to one day dance in *The Nutcracker*. I definitely remember feeling, 'Now this is what it feels like to really be a ballerina.'" Her whole family was in the audience on opening night, watching her dance on the very stage she once promised she'd be on.

BRAVO!

The Nutcracker dancers take their curtain call, bowing and curtsying for the audience. Do you think they did a great job? Well, then, stand up and clap loudly. Dancers absolutely love a standing ovation!

Pronunciation Guide

Allegro: ah-LAY-groh
Apotheosis: uh-PAH-thee-OH-suss
Arabesque: ahr-ah-BESK
Attitude: a-tee-TEWD
Balancé: ba-lahn-SAY
Balanchine: bal-UHN-cheen
Balletomane: buh-LEH-tuh-mein
Barre: bar
Cavalier: ka-vuh-leer
Celesta: suh-less-tuh
Coda: CO-dah
Commedia dell'arte:
   kuh-MAY-dee-uh del-AR-tee
Coqueluche: coke-loosh
Corps de ballet: core duh buh-LAY

Divertissements: dee-vehr-tees-MOHN
Drosselmeyer: Drahs-sul-my-yur
Duet: Dew-et
Dumas: Dew-MAH
En dedans: ahn duh-DAHN
En dehors: ahn duh-AWR
Enchaînement: ahn-shen-MOHN
Fouetté: fweh-TAY
Grand jeté: grahn zhuh-TAY
Jeté: zhuh-TAY
Libretto: luh-breh-tow
Mademoiselle: mad-mwuh-zel
Maillot: my-yoh
Mariinsky: mary-IN-skee
Mirliton: meer-luh-TOHN

Pantomime: pan-tuh-mime
Pas de deux: pah duh doo
Pirouette: peer-oh-wet
Plié: plee-AY
Polichinelles: poe-LEE-shee-NELL
Relevé: rel-uh-VAY
Rosin: rah-zin
Quatorze: ka-TORZ
Sauté: soh-TAY
Taglioni: TAL-yee-OH-nee
Tour en l'air: toor ahn lehr
Trepak: tray-pock
Tsar: zaar
Tulle: tool

Read More About It

Barton, Chris. *The Nutcracker Comes to America.* Minneapolis: Millbrook Press, 2015.

Bussell, Darcey. *The Ballet Book.* New York: Dorling Kindersley, 1994.

Fisher, Jennifer. *Nutcracker Nation.* New Haven, CT: Yale University Press, 2003.

Krista, Davida. *George Balanchine.* Minneapolis: Lerner Publications Company, 1996.

Lee, Laura. *A Child's Introduction to Ballet.* New York: Black Dog & Leventhal, 2007.

Levine, Robert. *A Child's Introduction to the Orchestra.* New York: Black Dog & Leventhal, 2001.

McCaughrean, Geraldine. *The Random House Book of Stories from the Ballet.* New York: Random House, 1994.

Newman, Barbara. *The Illustrated Book of Ballet Stories.* New York: Dorling Kindersley, 1997.

Wheeler, Opal. *Peter Tchaikovsky and the Nutcracker Ballet.* Akron, OH: Zeezok Publishing, 1959.

Index

Enjoy the rest of the Child's Introduction series!

A Child's Introduction to
African American History

A Child's Introduction
to Art

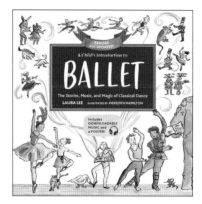

A Child's Introduction
to Ballet

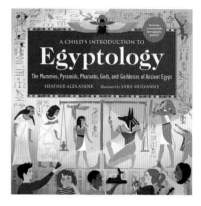

A Child's Introduction
to Egyptology

A Child's Introduction
to the Environment

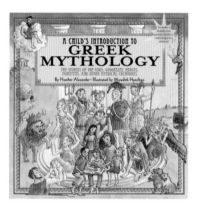

A Child's Introduction
to Greek Mythology

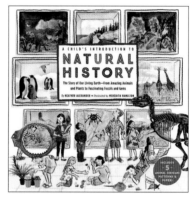

A Child's Introduction
to Natural History

A Child's Introduction
to the Night Sky

A Child's Introduction
to Norse Mythology

A Child's Introduction
to the Orchestra

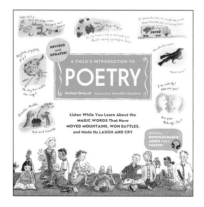

A Child's Introduction
to Poetry

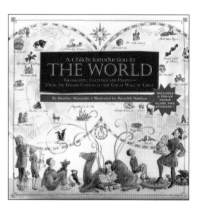

A Child's Introduction
to the World

BLACK DOG
& LEVENTHAL
PUBLISHERS

The Nutcracker